Use Hypnosis to Stop Smoking

Use Hypnosis to Stop Smoking

by Graham Old

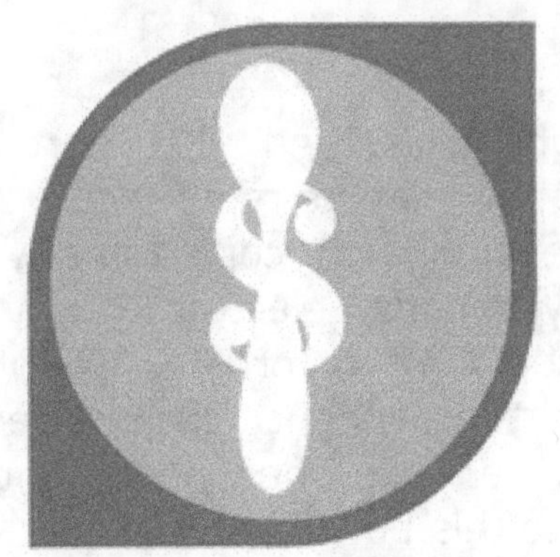

Use Hypnosis to Stop Smoking

Copyright © GRAHAM OLD

Published 2017 by Plastic Spoon

www.plasticspoon.info

Also by Graham Old

Fiction

Of Madness and Folly

The Removal

Pete, the Poet

Nonfiction

Mastering the Leisure Induction

Revisiting Hypnosis

The Elman Induction

The Hypnotic Handshakes

The Anxiety Guide

Acknowledgements

Helping someone to stop smoking is one of the greatest privileges afforded a hypnotist. I am grateful to each and every one of the clients who came to me to quit smoking.

The protocol that follows was developed over a number of years. It has been heavily influenced by the work of several other hypnotists, including but not limited to Stephen Brooks, Igor Ledochowski, John Cleesattel, Melissa Tiers, Roy Hunter, Jess Marion, Shawn and Sarah Carson and the late Jeffrey Stephens. I can fully recommend their work.

All Rights Reserved

Disclaimer

Any experimentation with the ideas presented in this book is undertaken at your own risk and responsibility. Nothing in this book should be taken as a replacement for seeking medical support, or training in psychotherapy.

Preface

This is the second book in our '*Use Hypnosis*' series of books.

The idea for the series arose due to the number of times we have been asked how to treat particular conditions. The question betrays a presumption that there is one correct way to treat the condition in question. This is, as far are we are concerned, an unhelpful way to view hypnosis *and human beings*!

There is no one answer to questions such as, "How do you treat blushing?" There are too many factors involved, which make each case unique. Yet, more than that, when it comes to actually working with people, we are doing precisely that – working with people, not issues.

Therefore, we have tended to avoid providing scripts to those who sought them from us. Instead, we have aimed to teach about the benefits of viewing each person as unique, moving beyond problems and teaching skills like acceptance, solution-focused practice and more. Nevertheless, this book – as with the other books in the series – is essentially a script with a very long introduction. So, how do we justify that?

Our scripts are not provided as one-size-fits all solutions. In fact, strictly speaking, they are not scripts at all. They are actually transcripts of a therapy session. The only changes that have been made are to make it more universally explicit, where it would have previously been focused on one person's situation.

We begin by looking at the issue in question, be that smoking, blushing or stress. We do not presume that the experience is the same for every person who faces such issues. Therefore, we spend some time looking at the nature of the issue and dealing with any necessary theoretical foundations. However, theory – particularly theories as to human psychology or the cause of human behaviours – is on the whole kept to a minimum.

We then look at the general approach that might be recommended in the majority of cases. This is not a 'do this, then do that…' exercise. Instead, we will share the range of ideas and techniques that we would consider, all things being equal. At all times, it is the responsibility of the reader to determine what does and does not apply in their situation.

Finally, we finish with the "script." This is most certainly not something that is just meant to be read to the person with the issue. The idea is for you to read through the script and note any areas where you can make it more specific or applicable in your case. The script is an example of the rest of the ideas in the book being put in to practice.

The feature that may make this series of books unique, compared to other hypnotherapy books, is that it is aimed both at hypnotists and their clients. If you are using these books for yourself, it would be recommended to read it through first, to note any areas where you can make it more specific to your unique experience. You can then record the script, making it more applicable to your circumstances.

The terminology in this book regularly shifts between 'you' and 'your client' to accommodate both sets of readers.

Contents

Introduction

This book roughly follows the direction that my Stop Smoking sessions take. The final hypnosis script then contains all of the ideas together in one place. However, that is not necessarily the way that I always work.

My style of practice is inherently solution-focused. So, I will always aim to spend the majority of a session being strengths-focused, resource-driven and future-oriented. That does not immediately come across in all of the sections leading up to the script. For example, it could appear that the Stop Smoking Strategy is a negative problem-focused example of aversion therapy. However, I should make clear that I only use that strategy with people who have already expressed some health concerns or have revealed that they have their own inner aversions. The strategy is then used to take them on a journey from that to choosing a positive outcome from quitting. The focus, looking at the bigger picture, is always solution-focused.

Exactly the same points could be made about the Goggle Box technique. On paper, it looks like an exercise in aversion. However, in reality, far more time is spent on the second "channel," where they are benefiting from being a non-smoker. Additionally, the time spent inhabiting their loved ones is often precious to people as they feel the care and affection – and later, pride and relief – that other people have for them.

So, as you read through the sections, be aware that the way they are presented is generally more positive than comes across on paper. And the script, which has been generalised to make it as applicable to as many people as possible, obviously loses all element of interaction and therefore misses many of the positive solution-focused comments that are dropped into the conversation. Hopefully, the general tone of the book and the presentation of the exercises helps to balance this out.

I am not at all suggesting that this is the only way to use hypnosis to stop smoking. In fact, as I alluded to in the acknowledgements, even this method builds on the work of numerous other people. However, this is the Brief Hypnosis approach and we have found it to be consistently effective and reliable and we share it in the anticipation that it will prove so for you and your clients too.

How to Use this Book

We are offering the techniques, ideas and suggestions in this book as an approach to use when working with those who desire to stop smoking. Not every idea will work for everyone. The only way to find what works well and what fits with your style of work is to put it into practice.

Although the hypnosis script contains all of our ideas and techniques in one place, it is not necessary to treat smokers in only one session. It is certainly possible, though if the smoker or therapist have misgivings over that, it is not essential. Over the years, I have adapted how many sessions I would see smokers for. Initially, it was always three sessions. Then, as some of the ideas in this book formed, I went down to one. I now give smokers the option of 1-3 sessions. By far the majority choose two sessions, though it is not rare for a smoker to want everything done and out of the way in one session. If two sessions are chosen, I may spend the first session on motivation, going through the intake and using the Goggle Box technique. The second session is then reserved for the Stop Smoking Strategy and the rest of what is seen in the Hypnosis Script. Alternatively, I may go through everything in the first session so they are a non-smoker from then. The second session is then used to strengthen and support their commitment.

My personal preference is to use the Goggle Box outside of hypnosis, as a motivation aid. I then use the Stop Smoking Strategy during hypnosis. However, I may bring them out slightly afterwards, before taking them back 'down,' as this has an intensifying effect on the experience. Both Goggle Box and the Stop Smoking Strategy can be used in or out of hypnosis. It is entirely your choice and flexibility is recommended.

The most beneficial way to make use of this book is to read it in order, finishing with the script. However, it is possible to work effectively using solely the Stop Smoking Strategy and the Hypnosis Script.

We do not recommend that you read the script verbatim to your client. It is meant to provoke ideas and demonstrate how we put some of our approach into action. A useful way to employ it is to read through, note which elements are useful and how it is structured. Then proceed with your own more tailor-made version. This is true also if you are planning to record the script to use for your own self-hypnosis.

GRAHAM OLD

Cravings Buster

I ask all of my clients to skip their last cigarette before coming to see me. For those who smoke a large amount, that may not have been a long time-gap since the previous cigarette, but it will seem like it to them.

I ask clients to skip a cigarette because I want to ensure that they come in with a craving for a cigarette. The first thing I do with them is remove their craving in a matter of minutes. This is a great convincer and serves to put them in a good head-space for carrying on with the session.

In the appendices, you will find five different cravings busters that you can use! I sometimes start with the dial to lower the craving and then move on to one of the others to eliminate it completely.

Bedside Manner

I want to briefly discuss the 'bedside manner' of a hypnotherapist during a smoking cessation session.

In the past, a hypnotherapist might present themselves as a person of authority. More than that, they are a person of authority employed to rid the smoker of their hideous habit. Aside from perpetuating a rather outdated model of hypnosis, such a position is at least a little lacking in empathy.

To my mind, the best image of the role of a hypnotherapist can be taken from the field of Acceptance and Commitment Therapy. In ACT, they use the metaphor of two people climbing two different mountains. As a therapist, it is not that I am a better climber than you, or have gone higher up the mountain. It is simply that from my standpoint, I can see some hazards and helps that you may not be aware of.

I think also of a scenario where someone may

knock on the front door having had one of their tyres blow-out. They may be perfectly capable of changing a tyre themselves, they simply do not have the necessary equipment. They do not need a lecture from you, or any patronising advice. They just need a bit of help and the loan of a jack and then they'll be on their way.

This scenario is useful as it addresses the attitude of the hypnotherapist towards their client. I would describe it as one of practical compassion. I see that my client has got themselves in a bit of a mess. I feel empathy for their situation. And I lend a practical hand to get them back on their feet. I am not their doctor, their preacher, their spouse, or their friend. I am simply someone who has the tools that they need at that point in time.

I would like to address one final element of the therapist's approach that I was pleased to see mentioned in *Quit* by Jess Marion, Shawn Carson and Sarah Carson. This is something that I refer to as being playfully provocative.

Playfully Provocative

Before I look at a client's list of fives, or between that and going through the intake form, I usually provide them with a brief warning. My wording usually goes something like this:

> H(ypnotist): "I should warn you that a previous client once referred to me as being… what was the phrase? Ah, 'playfully provocative.'"

> C(lient): "Really?"

> H: "I think what they meant by that is that I like to play Devil's advocate and sometimes I might push you to answer a question a bit more honestly or thoroughly, if I think you're holding out on me."

> [All of this is said with a slight smile on my face and a glint in my eye.]

> H: "So, if it ever seems to you like I am being a bit of a jerk, just presume it's all part of the therapy and we'll get along just fine!"

That last line usually elicits a smile from my clients. However, I still encounter scenarios where they underestimate the level of my 'provocation.'

I worked with one lady who had tried to quit numerous times. When I asked her how much she smoked, she laughed and said, "It's silly really... I only smoke ten a day." Throughout the rest of the intake, I used the word "silly" at different times, often with a slight chuckle.

At one point, she slammed her hand down on the desk and said, "It's not silly! This could kill me!" I stopped what I was doing and acted shocked before saying, "You are absolutely right. Let's take this seriously." She quit that session and remains smoke-free to this day.

So, even if you pre-warn clients that you may use humour and intentionally be provocative, some will still be surprised when you do! Nevertheless, I have found it to be a helpful part of my approach.

The fact is, we *are* talking about life and death matters. Yet, we are talking to people who have had that thrown in their face (think of tobacco packet pictures) for years and it has no effect. It can be useful to inject humour into such proceedings, as that can be a useful tool to enable you to make a serious point. However, more than that, playful provocation can act almost like a splash of cold water in the face. It can awaken someone to hard facts which they were either in denial about or had heard so many times in the same old way that they had no effect.

Joking about something as serious as smoking may seem like a strange thing to do. Yet, when handled skilfully, it can get through defences that have withstood all manner of rational arguments.

GRAHAM OLD

The Five Lists of Five

Prior to coming to work with me to quit smoking, I set my clients a task. I ask them to come to their session with five lists of (at least) five items. The lists are as follows:

1. A list of *at least* five reasons they want to be a non-smoker.

2. A list of all of the activities which they associate with smoking. They are asked to make this as complete as possible.

3. A list of their five highest values in life.

4. A list of the personal benefits they will enjoy one year after having given up smoking.

5. A list of all of the positives that they currently get from smoking.

The second list is the one that people tend to underestimate. Thus, it is emphasised that they should make this as complete as possible. Five would be an absolute minimum. When I give them the assignment, I usually suggest that they might want to make notes during the day as to what they were doing just before they had a cigarette.

These activities often function as triggers, which if they are not addressed can lead to psychological cravings. However, if the list is complete enough, there is no need for them to have a single craving.

The final list is the one that clients tend to struggle with the most. This may be because they are in a quitting mindset and do not want to allow themselves the luxury of thinking positively about smoking. However, they clearly get something out of it – even if it is just something for their fingers to do – or they would not need my assistance to stop smoking.

I ask them to imagine that there is a 'part' of them that wants to smoke and a 'part' that wants to quit. Most clients can readily make sense of this type of terminology, as it explains the struggle they've been dealing with in wanting to quit, but still feeling a pull to the cigarettes. I then ask them to imagine how the part of them that wants to quit smoking would answer the question. If he/she was allowed to speak for themselves, what would they say? Framed in such a way, most clients should be able to come up with at least 5 positives behind their smoking.

One of the things that thinking about these lists does is make a subconscious activity conscious. Most of the time a smoker lights-up they do so under the level of conscious awareness (i.e. subconsciously). To have to pause and think about their assignment causes them to think about their smoking in a way that they may never actually have done so before. Clients often come to their Stop Smoking sessions saying that they are now aware of every cigarette that they smoke. That makes your job a great deal easier!

Physical Phenomena

I do not usually recommend that hypnotists use "convincers" in their practice. I don't feel that they are necessary and they are usually designed in such a way to give the impression that the hypnotist is in control. I much prefer to proceed with the hypnosis and let phenomena occur naturally and organically.

However, smoking cessation may be considered a unique case. For some reason, smokers have bought into the fantasy that giving up is an incredibly difficult thing to do and that they are asking a great deal of you. I like to point out that most smokers have quit numerous times – and stayed quit beyond the point at which they are physically dependent on cigarettes. So, it is not quitting that is the problem. It is starting again!

Nevertheless, with smokers, I choose to employ 1 of 3 convincers, each of which involves their arm. I tell them that I am doing this to establish a connection with their subconscious mind and to get a feel for how willing their subconscious is to work with me. That is not strictly true, though I would pick up on any intentional resistance with these techniques.

1. Turning Round

The first exercise is incredibly simple, but when framed well can be powerful for clients to experience.

To start, have your client stand upright, with their feet together. Now ask them to stretch their right arm out in front of them, their right hand clenched into a fist, with their right thumb stuck up directly into the air. Then tell your client that on the count of 3 you want them to move their right arm around in a clockwise direction as far as they comfortably can, without moving their feet from the position they are currently in. They are told to stare at their thumb at all times whilst doing this and to tell you when they have reached the point where it becomes uncomfortable to move any further.

When they reach the point where they can move no further, ask them to stare past their thumb and almost imagine making a mark on the wall so they know how far they got.

The client is then told to resume their original position and put their arm down, but to close their eyes and imagine that it is still up in front of them. Ask them to imagine that they are once again rotating their body in a clockwise direction whilst staring at their thumb just like before. However, you ask them to imagine being able to move much further than before, both without discomfort and with the greatest of ease and speed. I sometimes say something like, "as if it was possible, you can even see yourself turning all of the way round." And then they are instructed to spin back to the beginning, drop their imaginary arm and open their eyes.

Then have them lift their right arm up as it was at the beginning and repeat the exercise, noting how much further than can turn, with much greater ease.

I tell my clients that this demonstrates that their imagination knew they were capable of more than they thought they were. I then congratulate them on having a powerful subconscious mind and say that I look forward to working with it.

2. Magnetic Hands

Here is a transcript of magnetic hands being used with a client:

Can I borrow you for a moment, to demonstrate the power of your mind? You'll enjoy it, trust me. All it really is, is a simple, fun, exercise that will show just what happens when you concentrate and focus, allowing your imagination to run free.

Okay, in a moment I'm going to ask you to close your eyes and place your hands out in front of you, like this.

[Demonstrate by placing your hands about 12 inches to a shoulder width apart, palms facing each other]

Then I want you to imagine that you have two powerful magnets strapped to the palms of your hands, pulling them together. When they touch, your head can simply fall forward as you relax.

So, now, place your hands out... and focus on the space between them... Now, close your eyes and imagine you have two powerful magnets strapped to the palms of your hands, pulling them together.

You can feel the force of that magnetic field between your hands, as you concentrate on that space between the palms [Wait for movement in the hands] ...that's right. Feel the pull. You don't have to force it. You don't have to fight it. Feel it now getting stronger and stronger. And the stronger it gets, the closer the hands come together... that's right... and the closer they get the stronger it becomes.

Just enjoy the power of your imagination, as you feel those magnets pulling the hands together, until they touch... Now... you can let your hands drop into your lap, as your head drops forward and you... relax.

I then have my client open their eyes and congratulate them on a focused and powerful subconscious. I explain that although there were no real magnets used, their subconscious was able to engage with my suggestions well enough to create a new reality for them. And that, I tell them, is the essence of hypnosis.

3. Unbendable Arm

The final 'convincer' that I may use is the unbendable arm. This simply consists of asking the client to stretch their arm out in front of them and to make a fist. Then tell them to make the arm as stiff and solid as they can, almost as if an iron rod ran through the inside of it. Ask them to make it so solid that you would not be able to bend it. Then attempt to bend their arm by moving their fist in towards their chest. Do not try *too* hard, as you do not want to succeed. However, you need to be convincing.

Then tell them that now they should make their arm so stiff and solid that even *they* wouldn't be able to bend it. Then say, "When you know that your arm is so stiff and solid that you won't be able to bend it, go ahead and try and find that it just gets more and more solid." If they have followed your instructions properly, they will not be able to bend their arm.

I then tell the client that they can stop trying, relax their arm and let it return to normal. I congratulate them on having a powerful subconscious that was even able to overpower their conscious efforts to bend their arm. I tell them that we are going to use that powerful subconscious to make solid unbendable changes in their life.

All three of these convincers, if presented poorly, could come across as gimmicky. However, the key is to frame them as a means of gaining information about your client's subconscious mind. That may be how powerful it is, how creative or focused it can be, or simply that it is willing to work with you.

The Intake

My usual intake form can be seen in the appendices. However, there are a number of questions that I wanted to highlight.

Some people, particularly those who roll their own cigarettes, may state that they are unaware how many cigarettes they smoke in a day. It is important to push them on this and encourage them to come up with an accurate figure. If it seems like they are merely guessing, it is likely that the actual figure is higher. If they take the time to work it out, you can be more confident in their accuracy.

Once we have a figure to work with, I then estimate how much someone is spending per month and per year on their smoking habit. (During this portion of the intake, I do intentionally refer to it as their 'smoking *habit*' as well, to highlight the unnecessary expense.) For some people, the figure will be meaningless, though if they've been smoking for decades that total can be calculated as well. Even those who are not short of money may feel unease at the amount spent, especially if this does not fit with their five stated highest values. For example, if they have spent nearly £30,000 over the last ten years and if they state that one of their values is being a good grandparent, I might say something like:

> H: "Now, if I knew you better, or if I was in a particularly provocative frame of mind, I might suggest that that's £30,000 you could have spent on your grandchildren!"
>
> C: *nods*
>
> H: "I won't tell them if you don't!"

If someone has been smoking for decades, they may claim to have forgotten why they started smoking. In that case, it can be helpful to have them think of the earliest cigarette they smoked and ask why they smoked that one. Then have them think of the cigarette before that. Carry on in this way until you are as close to their first cigarette as you can get. The chances are that they smoked that first early cigarette to fit in with the desired crowd, but it is always better to know for certain where possible.

One question that sometimes bemuses clients is 'How long does an average cigarette take you to smoke?' We ask this as when we are going through the form with the client, it allows us to have a conversation like so:

> H: "How long does an average cigarette take you to smoke?"

> C: "Um, I dunno. About 5 minutes?"

> H: "And how many of your 20 cigarettes would you say that you actually enjoy?"

> C: "Erm, maybe 2."

> H: "So, unless my calculator is faulty, that means you are spending £3000 a year – and shortening your life by nearly 25 days – for ten minutes enjoyment a day."

This is all said in a non-judgemental way, as if I am as surprised by the finding as them. I may continue:

H: "That must be an incredible ten minutes!"

They almost always respond:

C: "No, not really."

Nothing in the intake form is used to badger, embarrass, or judge clients. Instead, think of it as ammunition that you will provide *them* to assist with any ambivalence they may have about quitting.

Another question that some people stumble over, but which we shall soon see is useful, is asking about the impact of quitting on other people. In one sense, when a client says that it will not effect other people one way or another, it is a good sign. That means that they are there of their own accord, are not doing this to please or satisfy any one else and genuinely want to quit for their own reasons. However, it is also somewhat short-sighted of them to think that no one else will be impacted by their quitting. This can be a clue as to the same kind of ignorance that presumes smoking has no effect on anyone else.

I ask about anyone else who uses their car and is subject to the fumes in the car upholstery. I also inquire as to visitors to the home and if any of them will be less effected by smoke in the furniture. Even then, you may still encounter those smokers who insist that no one else is effected. I once worked with a grandfather who insisted that he did not smoke in the car and he also smoked in the garden at home. I asked if he ever held his grandchildren when he came in from the garden. He smiled as he said to me, "Yes, but the first thing I do after coming in doors is wash my hands." So, I asked if he also washed his hair and changed his clothes.

If encouraged in the right direction, almost everyone will be able to think of someone who will be impacted when they stop smoking. At the very least, this would be someone who is pleased that they may be around for a few more years.

The question, 'Why do you want to quit?' is always an interesting one. However, if their answer is generic or does not feel particularly heart-felt (for example, "I'm fed-up with the smell..."), then I ask an additional question that often sheds a great deal of light:

H: "Why do you want to quit _now_?

This question gets to the heart of why they want to quit and affords the therapist with some very useful information. Perhaps most significantly, it also reveals a live and heart-felt reason for why they really want to stop smoking.

If the reason given is any variation of 'Health Concerns,' then I prepare to engage in what I call anti-aversion therapy. This is outlined in the next chapter. However, I start by asking them to expand on their particular health concerns. I might also ask them questions to ascertain how aware they are of the dangers of smoking, though this is not usually necessary.

Anti-aversion Therapy

There is an approach to smoking cessation known as aversion therapy that remains popular in some quarters. When used in the context of smoking cessation, what this usually boils down to is a discussion or visualisation of all of the horrible ingredients in a cigarette and every possible negative consequence from smoking.

For quite some time, this was considered the most effective means of helping someone to quit. However, either smokers have changed over time, or therapists are paying more attention to their clients. For it is now widely agreed that aversion in and of itself is unlikely to be effective.

The problem is that nothing we as therapists say to our clients is likely to be news to them. They have seen the warnings on every pack of cigarettes. They have endured the persistent encouragements from their Doctor and family members to quit. They may even have known someone who died from smoking-related causes. The issue is, as we have previously suggested, smoking is a subconscious habit. They know all of this stuff consciously, but when it comes to lighting-up, it is an automatic action that takes places outside of the realm of rational thought.

That does not mean that I never discuss the downside of smoking. I simply do so within a wider context. If someone has come up with 5 reasons for quitting, as requested, it is rare that health concerns would not be one of them. If it is not, I might say something like:

> "I see that health concerns is not listed as one of your reasons for quitting. You've no idea what a pleasant change that makes. Smoker after smoker comes in here concerned about their health and I always think, 'If you were *that* concerned, you would just quit!' You know?

> "I mean, they know that cigarettes contain arsenic, cadmium (which you'll know is found in car batteries), amonia, butane (which I think is lighter fuel) and... What's the paint stripper one? Acetone. And so they know all about this and they're sitting in front of me saying they have some health concerns about

quitting. And I'm like, 'Er, you should!'

"You'd think it would make my job a hell of a lot easier, but the problem is that you lot know all this stuff nowadays. I used to scare people with horror stories of the effects of smoking. I had this list I used to go through:

• In any single year, at least 120,000 people in Britain will die from illnesses directly related to smoking

• Half of all teenagers now smoking will reach the age of 70. One quarter will lose 23 years of life expectancy

• In the last 50 years, an estimated 60 million people worldwide died as a result of smoking.

• Half of all smokers die prematurely

• A quarter of them die from lung cancer

"And in my head, my non-smoking head, that was all pretty conclusive, but I tell you what really changed my mind in a roundabout kind of way... It was this one young guy who said, 'can't you just make them taste like shit?' And I said, 'the trouble with that is, they already do!' And let's face it, if someone's gonna smoke arsenic and amonia, they'll smoke shit!

"So, I'm grateful that nowadays there are other techniques that we can rely on. There are dozens of health reasons not to smoke and everyone today knows these. So, I'd like to talk about *your* reasons for quitting, because these are far more interesting and they are going to be the main thing that drives you to put that old habit behind you..."

Is it an Addiction?

I have just referred to smoking as a habit. However, a number of clients that you see will speak of their "addiction." So, which is it?

The most helpful answer seems to be that smoking is both a *physical addiction* and a *psychological habit*. As you will know, cigarettes contain nicotine, which is an addictive substance. It is present in the tobacco leaf and when a cigarette is burnt, nicotine from the tobacco leaf is inhaled in cigarette smoke by the smoker. Nicotine enters the bloodstream via the lungs and reaches the brain within ten seconds of inhalation.

The nicotine from cigarettes provides a temporary high. Eliminating the regular fix of nicotine will cause a smoker to experience temporary physical withdrawal and cravings.

That being said, as far as addictions go, smoking is fairly mild. Few smokers light-up on an aeroplane, as they are able to wait until their flight comes to an end. Even fewer smokers wake up in the night with withdrawal symptoms. In fact, it is not at all rare – and I often use this example in my clinic – for a smoker to be so engrossed in some activity that they forget to smoke.

If a client comes in and speaks of smoking as an addiction, it is often a sign of how powerless they feel and how strong a grip they think cigarettes have on them. In such a situation, I will steer the conversation round to the aeroplane example above and suggest that thankfully our bodies seem capable of beating the addiction. However, apart from that, I will not challenge their choice of words. Over the years, I have found that it is an unnecessary battle to be having and can create a significant loss of rapport.[1]

On those occasions when I slip-up, perhaps by matching the clients choice of words and speaking of an addiction, I ensure that I later use the word 'habit' to balance the discussion.

Unless a client speaks of smoking as an addiction, I aim to introduce the language of 'habit' as early as possible. This is for a couple of reasons. Firstly, most people have had a habit that they grew out of. Secondly, although it may be difficult, we all know that habits (e.g. nail-biting) can be overcome. The idea of kicking the habit is almost inherent in the word.

---

1   The one alternative is when I am adding up the financial cost of their smoking. I intentionally use the language of habit then, as I am highlighting the decadence of the practice.

Goggle Box

The following text is written for the reader who is intending to stop smoking. However, it can be easily converted into a hypnosis script, as can be seen in our script at the end of the book.

I don't know if you're familiar with the TV show GoggleBox. It's a bizarre idea, which essentially involves the viewer watching groups of families and friends watching television. We cannot see what they are watching. We just see and hear their reactions. In this exercise, we are going to do something a little bit like that.

I would like you to start by thinking of those people for whom this decision to quit is meaningful. These are important people in your life, that will be positively impacted when you stop smoking. Think of between 1 and 4 people. And picture them on a sofa, sat looking at a television.

You cannot see what they are watching, but somehow you know that they are viewing you smoking. Except, they see it all, because they cannot hide from some of the facts and figures when it is right in front of them on TV, like smokers are prone to do. They notice everything, all the little details... good and bad.

They see the money that you are spending. Imagine that look on their faces, as they see you effectively roll up £10 notes and smoke them. Maybe they even call out to the TV screen to tell you to stop. And they see the effect that each individual cigarette has on your health, the effect of even one cigarette on your lungs. They see it all.

As they keep watching, they may see you getting ill. They might notice the first sign of that smoker's cough, or see you out of breath. They see you at the doctor's, getting results from your tests. They see everything that you have been ignoring.

You can see the sadness in their eyes.

They watch you go into hospital. They see you dying. They watch, heart-broken, as they know that there is nothing *they* can do about it. They see it all. They know where you're heading and what you are risking.

Now, I would like you to go ahead and float into one of them, so that you are watching through their eyes. Perhaps you are viewing the funeral even. Feel their love for you... Feel their love...

And now I would like you to float out and stand to one side of them. So, this time you can watch them watching you, but you can also see what is on that screen.

And watch as they get to switch channels and see an alternative outcome. They see you making the decision today to become a non-smoker. They see you re-learning to breathe fresh air. Did you see that look on their face?

They see how within 20 minutes of your last cigarette, your blood pressure re-adjusts to a normal level; your pulse drops to a normal level. They can see that after only 8 hours the Carbon monoxide levels in your blood drop to normal and the oxygen level in your blood increases to normal. After 24 hours - Chance of heart attack decreases.

As they reflect on this 24 hours, they notice the little things too. They notice an increased positivity, a boost in your self-confidence. Things that others may notice about you, without realising what it is you did to *bring about these changes today*. A sense of well-deserved pride in the decision you made.

See their faces as they keep watching... after 48 hours - Nerve endings start to re-grow; your ability to smell and taste things is enhanced. They can see it on your face as you're eating. You taste things in ways you hadn't done for years... It's all so fresh...

After 72 hours, your bronchial tubes relax and lung capacity increases. They see you, day by day, becoming more active.

They keep watching as, between 2 weeks and 3 months, your circulation improves; walking becomes easier; lung function increases by up to 40%. This is obvious to those around you, as they see your activity levels increase and the ease with which you move around... breathing smoothly, naturally and effortlessly.

They keep watching on. After 5 years - Risk of heart attack falls to about half that of a smoker. After 10 years, risk of heart attack falls to the same as someone who has never smoked.

See their faces as they watch this new life you make for yourself. And then pick someone and float into them and feel the connection they have with you... Maybe you can feel love, or pride, or relief, as they see you turn your life around... Watch that new you on the screen through their eyes as you live a long healthy, smoke-free life...

Now, float out of them and stand next to them. Then float back to your initial position, where you cannot see what is on the TV screen and you can leave them enjoying watching the new you, as you know that you now stand at a crossroads in your life.

The Stop Smoking Strategy

This Stop Smoking Strategy was taught by Stephen Brooks. It can be used in hypnosis or out of it. We provide an example of both. If you are planning to record this strategy and use it on yourself, it is recommended that you use the version within the hypnosis script.

The following transcript provides an example of the strategy being used outside of hypnosis. It can be seen that it is more conversational in this setting. (Text in bold is merely for the reader to keep track of where we are in the process.)

The strategy has four simple steps:

1. Trigger

The first step is usually a picture. In this picture, the client sees their hand reaching for a pack of cigarettes. If they roll their own cigarettes, you will want to swap this for a tobacco pouch. If you have a client who is a poor visualiser, you can use the feeling of reaching for a pack of cigarettes as the trigger.

2. Worst Consequence

The therapist then asks the client to let the picture/feeling of the pack of cigarettes fade into the background. He then asks the client to think of the worst consequence of continuing smoking. Usually when the therapist suggests how it could affect others the client experiences quite intense distress. This is more difficult to achieve with younger people, but still possible. You should reinforce the intensity of the feeling by either describing it in visual, auditory and kinaesthetic terms or by just talking about how awful it must feel.

3. The Statement: NO!

Have the client say the word "NO" out loud to themselves. By saying "NO," they are pushing the negative picture and feeling out of their mind. So, the picture change between this stage and the next is immediate, rather than the previous fading-out.

4. The Positive Benefits of Quitting

Here the client sees and feels the positive benefits of having said "NO" to the negative consequences of smoking. They should be encouraged to think of something that is strong enough to make them want to quit (i.e. not just the opposite of #2).

Break State

After the client has been through the four stages, they should 'break state.' This can be anything from asking them a nonsensical question, to simply having them open and close their eyes. This prevents the strategy from looping from #4 back to #1.

You will notice that this strategy – and especially, this example of it – includes a fair amount of aversion. We do not recommend this as a standalone strategy for that reason. However, in this case, the client was an older gentleman and had already indicated that health concerns were his primary reason for wanting to stop smoking. He also had in mind a clear picture of how he wanted to celebrate once he quit. That made the strategy particularly powerful for him.

H: "Now, before we carry on, I just need

to check a couple of things with you."

C: "Okay."

Information Gathering

H: "From what you've said, I think I already know the answer to this one, but what would be the worst possible consequence of continuing to smoke?"

C: "Well, an early grave, I suppose."

H: "So this is really a life or death situation in your mind?"

C: "Yes, definitely."

H: "And so the worst consequence would be the ultimate one – death. And I wonder, because obviously you're not around to grieve afterwards, what moment would be the worst for you personally?"

C: "Oh, I've thought about this a lot. It would be telling my children. Telling them that I've got lung cancer and seeing how crushed they are. And then I would be there feeling like it was my fault. I had caused this and I was taking away their dad and taking away their children's granddad."

H: "That's a powerful image."

C: "Yes, it is."

H: "Right, so let's look at the flip-side of that. What is the best positive benefit from giving up? Something that happens because you give up that is enough of a motivation to cause you to stop smoking right here and right now..."

C: "Well, we've seen how much I would save if I gave up. So, I would say, taking that money and treating the whole family to a holiday, that would only be possible if I gave up."

H: "That's almost like the opposite, isn't it? Celebrating life and your family."

C: "Absolutely."

H: "Okay, well, you can keep your eyes open, or close them for this bit. However you concentrate and focus is best."

[Client closes their eyes.]

H: "That's good... Now, I am going to teach you a simple 4-step process. And we are going to go through it a number of times, to make sure that we really get it fixed in your mind. Okay?"

C: "Yep."

H: "Great."

1. Trigger

H: "So, the first thing I would like you to do is to see, imagine or experience your hand reaching for a pack of cigarettes. And make the image close to you. See through your own eyes and feel your hand actually reaching out for that pack... And let me know when you've got that."

C: "Yep, got it."

2. Worst Consequence

H: "Okay, and now, as that hand reaches out, see that picture fade into the background and it is replaced by the worst possible consequence of you continuing to smoke. So, as you said, that's you having to tell your children that you have cancer. And you can get a feeling already for how painful that conversation would be, for how dreadful you would feel and you can see on their faces just how devastated they are. And of course, you may even feel ashamed, knowing that this could have been avoided.

"Let me know when you can really get a feeling for that awful situation."

[Client nods]

3. The Statement: NO!

H: "Okay, then when you know that you reject this awful scenario, that you say no to the idea of an early death and seeing your children suffer, I want you to go ahead and say the word "NO" out loud to yourself."

C: "No!"

H: "And that *No* pushes the negative picture and feeling out of your mind..."

4. Positive Benefit

H: "...to be replaced immediately by the positive benefit of saying no to smoking.

So, you can see your children and your grandchildren with you on that holiday of a lifetime. *Feel* that sense of pride in knowing that you did this. You stopped smoking and with the money you saved, you brought the whole family with you to celebrate this new life. This would not have been possible without that NO...

"See the picture clearly, vividly... hear the sounds, perhaps the sound of your grandchildren laughing and having fun... get a real sense of how wonderful that feels...

"Make it big, bright, vivid. See, hear and feel just how great that is. And as you watch your family celebrating, laughing and playing together, you can afford to give yourself a pat on the back. You did this. And it feels great."

[Client takes a deep breath and smiles]

Break State

H: "And you can now open your eyes."

[Client opens their eyes]

H: "So, that's easy enough, isn't it?"

C: "Yes."

H: "Do you think you've got those 4 stages?"

C: "Yes, I think so."

H: "Well, I'll take you through it once more, perhaps twice, and then we'll have you practice on your own..."

1. Trigger

H: "So, you can go ahead and close your eyes. And the first stage is to see, imagine or experience your hand reaching for a pack of cigarettes. See through your own eyes and feel your hand actually reaching out for that pack..."

2. Worst Consequence

H: "And now, as that hand reaches out, see that picture fade into the background and it is replaced by the worst possible consequence of you continuing to smoke. Telling your children that you have cancer. And get a feeling for how that would be. Really feel that."

[Client frowns]

3. The Statement: NO!

H: "And when you know that you reject this situation and choose to say 'no' to smoking, go ahead and say the word "NO" out loud to yourself."

C: "No!"

H: "And that No pushes the negative picture and feeling out of your mind..."

4. Positive Benefit

H: "...to be replaced immediately by the positive benefit of saying no to smoking. See your children and grandchildren with you on that holiday of a lifetime. *Feel* that sense of pride in knowing that *you did this*. Go for it... get a real sense of how wonderful that feels...

"*Really* feel it. Celebrate with your family."

[Client takes a deep breath and smiles]

Break State

H: "And you can open your eyes."

[Client opens their eyes]

H: "So, the four stages, as you've seen, are:

1. See your hand reaching for a pack

2. That image fades to be replaced by the worst negative consequences

3. You say No!

4. Immediately, that image switches to one of you enjoying the positive benefits of quitting.

H: "Okay, got that?"

C: "Yep."

H: "Now I'm going to be really patronising and ask you to repeat those four steps back to me."

C: "Okay...

1. See my hand reaching for a pack

2. Image fades to the worst negative consequences

3. I say a definite No!

4. The image immediately switches to one of me enjoying the positive benefits of quitting."

H: "Excellent. It's easy."

[Hypnotist counts off the steps on his fingers.]

1. See your hand reaching for a pack

2. That Image fades to the worst negative consequences

3. You say, No!

4. Image immediately switches to the positive benefits of quitting.

"You got it!"

[Client nods]

H: "So, I'm going to invite you to close your eyes and run through those 4 stages. And when you get to the end, you can open your eyes."

[Client closes their eyes. They frown, say "No" and then smile. They then open their eyes.]

H: "And again."

[Client closes their eyes. They frown, say "No," smile and open their eyes.]

H: "And again."

[Client closes their eyes. They frown, say "No," smile and open their eyes.]

H: "And once more."

[Client closes their eyes. They frown, say "No," smile and open their eyes.]

H: "Excellent. Well done... Now, tell me, how do you feel if you imagine yourself reaching forward for a packet of cigarettes?"

[Client leans back and puts their hand up.]

C: "Oh, no, no."

Taking Smoking A-Part

When you really think about it, smoking is a funny old habit. You take some paper, some leaves and some poison, light it, smoke that *and* inhale the fumes – and pay for the pleasure! In the cold light of day, there are not that many people who would deny that it is a strange thing to do.

And yet, hypnotherapists across the globe are kept busy by people who insist they want to stop smoking, but need some help. In a great deal of those cases, it is as if some part of the smoker wants to quit and some part wants to carry on smoking.

This is the reason that so many modern hypnotists employ protocols that use some version of parts work, whether it's an NLP *Six-Step Reframe*, John Cleesattel's *Manager's Meeting*, or Edwin Yager's *Subliminal Therapy*. The version you will find in our hypnosis script is closest in format to John Cleesattel's, yet has also been influenced by Yager.

The ambivalence that smokers can have should

not be mistaken for lack of motivation or commitment. If a client comes to see me and I believe they are not motivated enough to quit, I offer them a session to work solely on motivation. If they decline, or their motivation to quit does not increase, I do not take them on as a client. Ambivalence is a different matter.

A client can have extremely high motivation to quit and yet, at the same time, have a strong desire to keep smoking. It is the opposite or contradictory feelings towards smoking that define ambivalence and distinguish it from simply low motivation. This is a clear case where there are different 'parts' to a person, pursuing different ends.

In the appendices, you will see a description of the Visual Squash. This is an ideal NLP pattern to use when two distinct parts appear to be in conflict. It is also my technique of choice if all else fails.

Another reason that many modern smoking cessation protocols utilise parts-based approaches is to address the perceived benefits associated with smoking. This is obvious in something like the NLP Six-Step Reframe, where you seek out the positive intention behind each part's behaviour. Within the Hypnosis Script, you will see our version of something similar where we encourage the client to openly think of the positive benefits they got from their smoking. One reason that the old-fashioned aversion-based approaches would often fall down was because they underestimated the pros of smoking, for the client. We talk openly about the apparent benefits and address any gaps that may be left by their absence. This is a useful means of lessening the risk of cravings, as the desire behind the desire for cigarettes is being met in a new way.

If you choose to use the approach shown in our hypnosis script, I would encourage you to be flexible with it. It is also worth familiarising yourself with other parts-based models, so that you can chop and change if and when it feels appropriate. The key ideas are i) acknowledging ambivalence through the recognition of different 'parts' and ii) recognising and replacing the benefits that smoking brought into the smoker's life.

GRAHAM OLD

Stop Smoking Hypnosis Script

Preamble

This script is not intended to be read as it is, word for word. Instead, it is an example of the approach in this book being used in action. It is preferable if you take this transcript, learn from it and then write your own.

Words in italics should receive a different emphases. Words in bold are simply headings for the reader to know where they are in the script.

Elipses [...] indicate a pause, whereas square brackets [] are directions for the hypnotist to take note of.

The Stop Smoking Hypnosis script contains the following elements:

- Induction (involving arm levitation or catalepsy)

- Goggle Box (if not already used)

- The Stop Smoking Strategy (if not already

used)

- Values-Based Alternatives

- Direct Suggestions

- Time-Travel

There are a number of points here which may benefit from further explanation. The induction intentionally utilises physical phenomena. If you are recording the induction to use as a self-hypnosis resource, that may be less than useful. In that case, you might want to use the induction in the appendices.

We believe that this is the first time that the Modified Wicks Induction has been seen in print. However, if you are more familiar with an alternative induction that uses catalepsy, levitation, or other physical phenomena involving the arm, you are of course more than welcome to use that instead.

We looked at utilising the perspective of loved ones earlier, in the Goggle Box chapter. My preference is to use it as a means of helping a smoker finalise their decision to quit. However, it is possible to use it as the first part of the hypnosis script. That would be advisable if the script is being recorded for self-hypnosis.

Finally, the Stop Smoking Strategy can be used in or out of hypnosis. Some therapists like to use it before hypnosis begins, as a means of cementing the smoker's decision and prepare for hypnosis. My preference is to use it within hypnosis.

Induction (Modified Wicks Induction)

H: "Are you left-handed or right-handed?"

C: "Right-handed."

H: "Okay, well let's use your left arm then, just to give it a bit more attention. You're okay if I touch your arm or wrist."

[Said as a statement, not a question.]

C: "Yeah."

H: "Any issues with your arm, wrist, elbow or shoulder?"

C: "Nope."

H: "And, finally, do you have any objections to going into hypnosis quickly?"

C: "No."

H: [Takes the client's arm by the wrist and extends arm all the way above the head...]

"Close your eyes. Take a deep breath. Hold it..."

[As the hypnotist says, "hold it," they let go of the arm almost completely, with it just about resting on their thumb.]

H: "Let the breath out. And let the rest of your body relax completely...

"In a moment, *not yet*, but in a

moment..."

[Hypnotist removes thumb from under the wrist imperceptibly, until the arm is resting in the air on its own.]

H: "...your arm will slowly begin to float down to your lap. As it comes down, you will feel yourself going more and more deeply into hypnosis. But I don't want you to go all the way in, until that hand has come to rest."

[The arm begins to float down.]

H: "That's right, coming down only as quickly as you go deeper into hypnosis. The deeper you go, the better you feel. And the better you feel, the deeper you go. All the way..."

[Once the hand has come to rest in their lap or by their side, the hypnotist says:]

H: "And you can go all of the way inside now. Every beat of your heart, every word that I say and every sound that you hear, causing you to go deeper and deeper."

Goggle Box

"I would like you to start by thinking of those people for whom this decision to quit is meaningful. These are important people in your life, that will be positively impacted when you stop smoking. Think of between 1 and 4 people. And picture them on a sofa, sat looking at a television.

"You cannot see what they are watching, but somehow you know that they are viewing you smoking. Except, they see it all, because they cannot hide from some of the facts and figures when it is right in front of them on TV, like smokers are prone to do. They notice everything, all the little details... good and bad.

"They see the money that you are spending. Imagine that look on their faces, as they see you effectively roll up £10 notes and smoke them. Maybe they even call out to the TV screen to tell you to stop. And they see the effect that each individual cigarette has on your health, the effect of even one cigarette on your lungs. They see it all.

"As they keep watching, they may see you getting ill. They might notice the first sign of that smoker's cough, or see you out of breath. They see you at the doctor's, getting results from your tests. They see everything that you have been ignoring.

"You can see the sadness in their eyes.

"They watch you go into hospital. They see you dying. They watch, heart-broken, as they know that there is nothing they can do about it.

"They see it all. They know where you're heading and what you are risking.

"Now, I would like you to go ahead and float into one of them, so that you are watching through their eyes. Perhaps you are viewing the funeral even. Feel their love for you... Feel their love...

... ...

"And now I would like you to float out and stand to one side of them. So, this time you can watch them watching you, but you can also see what is on that screen.

"And watch as they get to switch channels and see an alternative outcome. They see you making the decision today to become a non-smoker. They see you re-learning to breathe fresh air. Did you see that look on their face?

"They see how within 20 minutes of your last cigarette, your blood pressure re-adjusts to a normal level; your pulse drops to a normal level. They can see that after only 8 hours the Carbon monoxide levels in your blood drop to normal and the oxygen level in your blood increases to normal. After 24 hours - Chance of heart attack decreases.

"As they reflect on this 24 hours, they notice the little things too. They notice an increased positivity, a boost in your self-confidence. Things that others may notice about you, without realising what it is you did to *bring about these changes today*. A sense of well-deserved pride in the decision you made.

"See their faces as they keep watching... after 48 hours - Nerve endings start to re-grow; your ability to smell and taste things is enhanced. They can see it on your face as you're eating. You taste things in ways you hadn't done for years... It's all so fresh...

"After 72 hours, your bronchial tubes relax and lung capacity increases. They see you, day by day, becoming more active.

"They keep watching as, between 2 weeks and 3 months, your circulation improves; walking becomes easier; lung function increases by up to 40%. This is obvious to those around you, as they see your activity levels increase and the ease with which you move around... breathing smoothly, naturally and effortlessly.

"They keep watching on. After 5 years - Risk of heart attack falls to about half that of a smoker. After 10 years, risk of heart attack falls to the same as someone who has never smoked.

"See their faces as they watch this new life you made for yourself. And then pick someone and float into them and feel the connection they have with you... Maybe you can feel love, or pride, or relief, as they see you turn your life around... Watch that new you on the screen through their eyes as you live a long healthy, smoke-free life...

"Now, float out of them and stand next to them. Then float back to your initial position, where you cannot see what is on the TV screen and you can leave them enjoying watching the new you, as you know that you now stand at a crossroads in your life."

The Stop Smoking Strategy

"I would like you now to see, imagine or experience your hand reaching for a pack of cigarettes. Or if you roll your own, see a tobacco pouch. And make the image close to you. See through your own eyes and feel your hand actually reaching out for that pack... And let your head nod when you've got that."

[Client nods]

H: "Okay, and now, as that hand reaches out, see that picture fade into the background and it is replaced by the worst possible consequence of you continuing to smoke. That may be having a heart attack, or getting lung cancer. Or it might be not living to walk your daughter down the aisle, or see your children grow-up. Whatever it might be, the worst possible consequence of you continuing to smoke...

"Nod your head when you can really get a feeling for that awful situation."

[Client nods]

H: "Okay, then when you know that *you reject this awful scenario*, that you say no to the idea of an early death and seeing your children suffer, I want you to go ahead and say the word "NO" either in your head or out-loud."

C: "No!"

H: "And that 'No' pushes the negative picture and feeling out of your mind...

H: "...to be replaced immediately by the positive benefits of saying no to smoking. And there are so many benefits... perhaps you focus on the positive effect on your health, or the financial benefits, or removing the smell of cigarettes, or the example you will set to others, or the prolonged life... so many positive outcomes... if it's at all possible, let your mind focus on just one, the greatest positive benefit, and make it a big one.

"If it's financial, see what you will buy with the money you save... if it's health, see yourself running or jumping or just generally being the specimen of good health. Make the image vivid and big... And really *feel the surge of pride and satisfaction*, knowing that your decision brought about that positive outcome.

H: "And you can now open your eyes."

[Client opens their eyes]

H: "And close them again."

[Client closes their eyes]

H: "I'll take you through this a couple more times, to ensure that it is fixed in your mind. "

"So, the first stage is to see, imagine or experience your hand reaching for a pack of cigarettes. See through your own eyes and feel your hand actually reaching out for that pack...

"And now, as that hand reaches out, see that picture fade into the background and it is replaced by the worst possible consequence of you continuing to smoke. Don't go easy on yourself. Really get a feeling for how that would be. Really feel that.

"And when you know that you reject this

situation and choose to say 'no' to smoking, go ahead and say the word "NO" out loud or to yourself."

C: "No!"

H: "And that 'No' pushes the negative picture and feeling out of your mind...

"...to be replaced immediately by the positive benefit of saying no to smoking. Feel that sense of pride in knowing that you did this. Go for it... get a real sense of how wonderful that feels...

"And you can now open your eyes."

[Client opens their eyes]

H: "And close them again."

[Client closes their eyes]

H: "Imagine or experience your hand reaching for a pack of cigarettes. See through your own eyes and feel your hand reaching out for that pack...

"And now, as that hand reaches out, see that picture fade into the background as it is replaced by the worst possible consequence of you continuing to smoke. Really feel that.

"And when you know that you reject this situation and choose to say 'no' to smoking, firmly say the word "NO" out loud or to yourself."

C: "No!"

H: "And that 'No' pushes the negative picture and feeling out of your mind...

H: "...to be replaced *immediately* by the positive benefit of saying no to smoking.

Make that image big, bold and bright. And really feel it. Feel that sense of pride in knowing that you did this. Get a real sense of just how wonderful that feels..."

H: "And you can open your eyes."

[Client opens their eyes]

H: "And close them again."

[Client closes their eyes]

Values Based Alternatives[2]

H: "And now you can just take a nice deep breath and relax... Getting used to taking a nice breath of fresh air... And I wonder now if you could visualize, imagine or experience a conference room. This will be a meeting room with a conference table and chairs, and you sitting at the table.

---

2 Some elements in this section are taken from John Cleesattel's *Stop Smoking Protocol*. They are used here with kind permission.

"Nod your head when you have that."

[Client nods]

H: "Then the first thing I would like you to do is invite to this meeting your smoking activity. And that means different things to different people. To some people it means 'the part of you that makes you smoke,' to others it means simply you smoking, or the younger you who started this habit, others visualise a cigarette. Whatever it means to you, I would like you to invite to the meeting, your smoking activity.

"Invite them to the meeting, perhaps even to sit next to you, and let me know when they arrive."

[Client nods]

"And what we are going to do here is

something quite unusual for a stop smoking program. We are going to discuss some of the positives of you smoking. These don't necessarily need to be genuine positives, but they appear that way to the part of you that smokes. They are the reasons that you have smoked."

[Turn to the list of the positives that they said they currently get from smoking and insert one into the paragraph below.]

"For example, you have said that you smoke to help you relax. Now, I would like your subconscious mind to come up with an alternative activity that is better for you, that you will enjoy, that can help you relax. There could even be more than one, there could be half a dozen, ten, twenty alternative activities that your subconscious mind can come up with that you will enjoy more, that will be better for you and that will help you relax even more... taking a deep breath, going for a walk, doing yoga, for example, but for now focus in on just one... one out of many... And have that activity also join you at the table.

"Now think of something else that smoking does for you, something that that smoking part of you might perceive to be a positive, like getting you in with the cool kids. And I would like your subconscious to come up with an alternative activity, at least one, to meet whatever need that is. And have that positive activity take a seat at the table.

"And as you carry on, in your own time now, you might notice that that smoking activity begins to fade, or shrink somewhat. Some people even say that it skulks out of the room once it realises that it is no longer needed. Just keep going in your own time, accepting the apparent positives that that smoking activity gave you and coming up with better alternatives. We're not denying those needs – we're meeting them in better ways.

"In fact, as we continue, your subconscious can take care of choosing alternatives for the other benefits that you once thought smoking brought you. You don't even need to consciously be aware of all of the alternatives that your subconscious comes up with. It can be a nice surprise as you see them taking root in your life.

Now, if there is any part of your smoking activity left, you can invite it to either leave the room, or to accept a new role. Let me know which option it chooses.

[Client answers. If the smoking activity chooses to leave, invite the client's inner "boss," the part of them that likes to be in charge, to join you at the table. If all else fails, invite their subconscious to take charge. Otherwise, continue as below.]

"That activity has stuck with you through thick and thin and had been difficult for you to shift. So, to provide it with a new need to meet, I am going to invite that old smoking part of you to become your new coach. It will need to employ all of its stubbornness and persistence to keep you committed to the new activities you have chosen. Let me know when it accepts its new role."

[Client nods]

"And you can go ahead and picture it or symbolise it in a new way.

"This action team that you have assembled round the table are empowered by your 5 highest values of [name the client's top 5 values]. They are the things that your coach will use to motivate you and drive you forward into the happier, healthier you. And they will help you to form new associations as you enjoy a new happier healthier lifestyle.

"Instead of [name association from client's list], you may [name alternative]."

[For example, instead of smoking when you enjoy a pint, you can appreciate not having to go outside and stay to enjoy the conversations you're having. Instead of smoking when you drive, like you used to, your action team can assist you to enjoy the fresh air, without worrying about taking your eyes off of the road, or dropping ash on yourself...]

"And as you *find yourself*... living a life according to your highest values... you are going to *discover a fresh level of satisfaction* like you have never known. The journey that you are now on, the new route that you are taking, will be one of vitality and health and joy... You have done so much more than *quit smoking*. You have reclaimed your life from the tobacco barons who would have had you smoke your health and money all away... you've reclaimed your life and rededicated it to these five values... and that is exciting... and you can wonder just what you will discover about yourself in the coming weeks and months, as you *redesign your life* and rediscover a sense of fun and freedom, in place of smoke and ash... Freedom to *lead that life defined by your values...*"

Direct Suggestions

"One of the things that may surprise you about your new life is that fresh spring that you notice in your step. That little clue, just for you, that things are moving in a positive direction.

"And because you will *find that fulfilling*, there will be no desire or temptation to sabotage your progress in any way, shape or form.

"You may find some people who struggle to believe that you are now smoke-free... as they see how straightforward and effortless it appears for you... But you can choose how much time you do or do not spend with them. You will have no desire to subject yourself to needless temptation.

"You will find, contrary to the expectations of such naysayers, that you will not gain any unhealthy weight as a result of stopping smoking. In fact, because you can now taste your food properly, without a mouth coated in tar, you will find that you now eat so much more mindfully. You do not eat simply to finish a meal, but you take the time to enjoy every mouthful, every chew.

"This will be the direction that your life takes from here onwards... a life a genuine satisfaction... a life of value and integrity."

Time-Travel[3]

"I would like you now to travel a year into the future... a year from today... you have been a successful non-smoker for a whole year. And you... feel... great!

"You know the benefits you enjoy as a non-smoker... You knew what they would be before you even began this journey. "Just imagine them now..."

---

3 Some elements and wording in this section are taken from Roy Hunter's *Benefits Approach*. They are reproduced here with kind permission.

[Read each benefit from the list of five, allowing a few seconds for the client to imagine each one...]

"If you choose these benefits for yourself, then indicate that choice right now by taking one deep breath...

"That's it... The replacement for yesterday's breath of smoke is one deep breath of air.

"And you may notice as you see yourself here in the future, that any thought of smoking is a completely alien idea to you. You are a non-smoker. Perhaps go back 6 months, so you are now 6 months from the time you stopped smoking. Notice that you look healthier. Your skin, your breathing, your voice... clearer, fresher... like the air that you breathe. Go back in time again so that you are only 3 months from the day that you became a non-smoker. Notice that you can already see, experience and enjoy the benefits of being a non-smoker.

"Now go back 10 weeks, so you are only 2 weeks from when you stopped smoking. You've already started saving money. Breathing more easily as you walk about. That smile on your face, so pleased and justifiably proud of the life-changing decision that you made. Notice how any time you are in a situation where you would have previously reached for a cigarette, the idea does not occur to you. Your subconscious mind has made new associations... more fulfilling ways to meet those needs. And see how any time you might have been tempted previously, you now simply take a nice deep breath of fresh air and focus your mind instead on the benefits that you are already enjoying now that you are a non-smoker... *Enjoy them now*.

"And in fact, you can go back now to your very first cigarette. Just go ahead and ask your subconscious mind to take you back and travel back to that first cigarette... If you find that the first one is not memorable to you, you can simply go to the first one that you remember... And go there now with all of the knowledge that you now have. And step into that younger you and see through their eyes. And as they go to accept a cigarette, you can stop them. You can stop them with all of the knowledge and wisdom and resources and power of choice that you now have. Let them know, let them become aware, allow them to realise in no uncertain terms what a bad idea it would be to smoke that cigarette... how it is not actually what they want to do... how that need can and will be met in better ways... And you can take a nice deep breath and reject that first cigarette. And as you do so, you can even let that memory fade like a wisp of smoke.

"I don't know whether you will refuse it, or snap it in two, or throw it on the floor and stamp on it... However you want to reject it is fine... but you do so because you choose these benefits instead... and you choose to live with a decision that will make you happier and healthier... and you feel great about that.

"And see yourself, or imagine yourself, moving on to what would have been your second cigarette... And with all of your knowledge and wisdom and freedom of choice now, you can reject that too... And the next. Feeling better and better as you do so. And the next. And the one after that. In fact, your subconscious mind can operate at a level much quicker than your conscious mind, so allow your subconscious to work away in the background, as we carry on, rejecting, refusing, removing the memory of every cigarette you ever smoked.

"Whenever you use your power of choice to focus your mind on the benefits you choose, yesterday's old urges are simply forgotten... vanishing into the mists of time, replaced with your new friend, freedom... to focus your mind, thoughts or actions on whatever you choose, whether at work or play, at home or away from home, alone or with others. You have the power of choice. You love your power of choice, and it was your choice to become a non-smoker... And your decision is bringing you the benefits you have chosen... so just imagine them vividly...

"And imagine your most important benefit so vividly that you feel as though you already enjoy success. Imagine that and really get a feel for it. Be glad. Imagine your benefits so vividly... that you feel as though *you already enjoy success*!

"And that new you, that path you have chosen to walk today, is reinforced and remembered and yes re-celebrated each time you take a nice deep breath of fresh air...

"See yourself a year from now, smoke free, healthy, happy, enjoying life more than you ever thought possible.

"You still see other people that smoke, but now you feel sorry for them. And you can be thankful that that is not you, as you see them banished to the outside, a slave to their cigarettes.

"Realize now that you really are a non-smoker, and it feels great! See yourself now a non-smoker. No longer a victim, no longer a slave.

"No! You have decided! You are a non-smoker, and you now realize that it is the best decision you ever made. And that can feel so good.

"So you can declare out-loud to yourself now:

I am a non-smoker.

I am a non-smoker.

I *am* a non-smoker.

I am a *non*-smoker.

I am a non-smoker!

[This is said to them at least 5 times, if not more, each time with more and more conviction.]

"And the moment, the very moment that

you are ready to begin this new life, this fresh, fulfilled life, you can take a nice deep breath and open your eyes."

[Client takes a deep breath and opens their eyes.]

"Congratulations!"

End of Session Guidance

After I have gone through a hypnosis session with someone to stop smoking, I usually take a few moments to share some tips with them. I give these as a hand-out as well, but clients tend to still be suggestible for the first few moments after coming out of hypnosis. So, it is a good time to share the following.

The first thing I do is ask them how it feels to be a non-smoker. They almost always say "great!" I then ask them if they want a cigarette and they always say, "No!" I then welcome them to their life as a non-smoker.

I provide each client with the following information and tools for continued success:

Rubber Band

I explain that for around 5% of people, they have a few cravings as the nicotine leaves their body over the next 3 days. So, I provide them with a rubber band to wear on their wrist, which I suggest they probably won't need. Whenever they even think about smoking, I advise them, snap it so it stings. They will find that this will stop them from even thinking about it!

Pubs and Clubs

It is a personal decision, but some people choose to stay away from pubs and clubs for a couple of weeks. Alcohol lowers inhibitions and people associate drinking with smoking.

Do Not Test Yourself

I encourage people not to needlessly test themselves, or allow friends to do it to them. That would be like eating an enormous cream cake to see if your diet is working. It is unnecessary and illogical. You can see it is working from the fact that you are now a non-smoker and therefore not smoking!

Air Freshener

I suggest that my clients get some air freshener to kill the stench that smoking has given everything they own. They are usually surprised by how much they smell smoke the way that all other non-smokers do, and *it does stink*.

This is usually the extent of the advice that I share just after the session. The information that I send them home with can be seen in the appendices.

GRAHAM OLD

Appendix A - Cravings Busters

1. Dial it Down

Feel a craving and notice where in your body it is. Pay more careful attention to it than you usually do. It is not merely a "I must have this!" sensation. You might be able to locate it in a specific part of your body, or note a size or colour that it has.

Then scale your craving from 1-10.

Now imagine an enormous volume control in front of you, as big as your torso. Imagine that the volume is set at the number you scaled your craving to be.

Then, just for a second, turn the volume up slightly. Notice as the craving increases. It may grow in size, or change colour, or you may just feel it more intensely.

Now, turn the volume back down to the original number you scaled.

Then, turn the number down further, allowing yourself to feel the changes to your craving as you do so.

You may choose to dial down to a manageable number, like 2. Or you might dial it down to 5 and then use one of the other cravings busters to remove it completely. Or you could just turn the volume all of the way down to zero.

2. Objectifying the Urge

This technique, from John Cleesattel, uses your imagination to visualize the craving and give it physical properties. By doing so, it changes it from a feeling, to an object. When we get rid of the object, the feeling is gone also.

Please close your eyes and visualise the unwanted feelings or craving.

- Show me with your hands, how big is it?

- If you could assign a colour to it, what colour would it be? What colour would *happy* and *no worries* be?

- If you were to pick it up, would the craving be heavy or light?

- What shape is it? (Round, square, triangle...etc)

- Is it solid or transparent?

- Is the surface of it rough or smooth?

- Is the surface warm or cold?

- Take the object and put it in a strong box, then seal the box closed in a manner in which you are sure the box cannot be opened. You can lock it, tie it, chain it, weld it, etc. Just as long as you are *sure* the box will not open. Let me know when you have done this.

- Take the box and move it to the other side of the room (or push it off a cliff, etc). When you have done this, open your eyes.

- Now, try to find that feeling.

3. Reverse Spin

- Direct your focus of attention to your body. Notice your internal bodily sensations for a moment.

- Think about your craving and notice the movement of that feeling (it will probably start in your stomach and move upwards towards your head or mouth).

- Using your powers of imagination, take this feeling out of your body and in your mind's eye see it spinning in front of you like a wheel.

- Then imagine what colour it is and change the colour to something more pleasing.

- Then reverse the direction of the spin perhaps by turning the wheel upside down so that the wheel is spinning in the opposite direction directly in front of you.

- Then pull the spinning wheel back into you.

- Continue spinning the feeling in the opposite direction. The feeling should now be moving down through your throat into your chest and stomach, i.e down instead of up.

- Spin the feeling faster and faster until it reduces and / or eventually disappears.

4. The Drop Through Technique

Recognise that whatever you resist persists. Like all of the cravings busters in this appendix, this one begins by having you accept and acknowledge your craving.

- Focus on the sense that tells you that you want a cigarette.

- Divide that sensation in half. Then in half again.

- "Drop through" that feeling and see what is beyond it.

- Whatever new feeling comes up, drop through it to see what is beyond that.

- Keep going until you feel a clear state of mind.

- Give yourself a pat on the back!

5. Increase the Urge

I would not use this technique with someone when they first come into my office. This is more useful as a craving buster to have in their toolbox for after they have quit, if they ever need it.

This technique could not be more simple.

Feel the craving and – as with Objectifying the Urge – get a real sense for it in terms of size, etc.

Then increase the craving.

Invite it to get stronger and stronger and fill your body.

Some people find that the craving fades within a matter of seconds, but you don't want that. The idea here is to tough it out and really experience the wave of a craving.

Within five minutes, your craving will pass.

Each time you try this technique, the cravings will pass more and more quickly.

Appendix B – Intake Form

1) Name

2) Contact Details

3) Date of Birth

4) How much do you smoke?

5) Do you smoke anything other than cigarettes?
- ☐ Cannabis
- ☐ Cigars
- ☐ E-cigs
- ☐ Vapes

6) When did you start smoking?

7) Why did you start smoking?

8) What do you think needs to be done for you to permanently quit?

9) Why do you want to quit smoking?

10) How long does an average cigarette take you to smoke?

11) What was the best experience of you entire life?

12) What was the worst experience of your entire life?

13) Who else will be effected by your decision to stop smoking today?

14) Do you live with anyone who smokes?

15) Have you tried any other alternative therapies to cure this problem before?

16) Have you got any questions for the hypnotherapist before we begin?

Appendix C – Alternative Induction

The following induction, a variation of the Dr. Flowers Induction, can be used as an alternative to the one in the hypnosis script. If you are working with a client, then it is recommended that you use an induction that utilises catalepsy or levitation of the arm. However, if you are recording the script for the purposes of self-hypnosis, the following induction will suffice.

H: "Go ahead and get yourself comfortable. Your arms and legs uncrossed and your hands perhaps resting on your lap, or by your side.

"And I would like you to fix your eyes on a spot on the wall in front of you. Then, soften your eyes… as though you are looking through the wall… at a very pleasant scene…

"Look at the scene in a vague, dreamy kind of way...

"In a moment, you can allow yourself to find all of the muscle groups in your body relaxing... Allow your facial muscles to relax... Your arms can relax... your legs... Your whole body can let go...

"And soon you will close your eyes and drift into a nice peaceful hypnotic rest.

"In a moment, I'm going to count from one to twenty. On each count, I want you to close your eyes... And in between counts, you can open your eyes...

"And sometime before I reach the count of twenty... Maybe at fifteen, maybe at ten... Maybe even at five... You'll close your eyes... and *go into a deep, sound hypnotic rest*.

"So, I will say 'One' and you will close your eyes. And then you will open them again. Then I'll say 'Two' and you will close your eyes and so on.

"As you continue to gaze peacefully at that pleasant scene through the wall, you can begin to notice as your body relaxes. You can notice the tendency for your body to relax and you can let it do so. The muscle groups in your face relaxing... your arms relaxing... your legs... your whole body can let go and relax completely...

"As I begin to count:

"One... Two... Already noticing a tendency for the eyes to want to stay shut...

"Three... Four... As if your eyes are heavy and would rather stay shut....

"Five... Six... Your whole body sinking further into that deep relaxation...

"Seven... Eight... Doubling that relaxation with every number I count...

"Nine... Ten... Picturing that peaceful scene...

"Eleven... Twelve... And if your eyes are still open, you can notice that feeling almost like glue each time you try to open those heavy eyes...

"Thirteen... Fourteen... And if your eyes are already shut, you can simply relax further with each number...

"Fifteen... Sixteen... Deeper and deeper...

"Seventeen... Eighteen... Doubling that relaxation

"Nineteen... and Twenty... Allowing your eyes to stay closed now, as you drift into that peaceful scene and enjoy the serenity... Enjoy the rest..."

Appendix D – The Visual Squash

If someone comes back for a second session and they have been smoking in-between sessions, it is necessary to find out why they smoked.

You may be surprised by how many people say they did it to test if the hypnosis was working. You can point out to them that it was working just fine until they did that! Such people can be hypnotised again, perhaps simply with the Stop Smoking Strategy or the Goggle Box. Additionally, include suggestions that they will have no need to test the work, as their continued non-smoking is evidence of their powerful subconscious mind's ability to discard old habits.

It is always a good idea to remind people that hypnosis is not magic. I always tell clients that my job is to empower *them* to do the work. That seems to remove the need to test whether the hypnosis has been effective.

Some people smoke because an association was missed. Perhaps they had a strong association with smoking and driving that they had failed to alert you to. These people can be hypnotised with the fresh information you have and taken through the Values Based Alternatives portion of the hypnosis script. You may also want to repeat the Direct Suggestions and Time-Travel elements of the script.

Other people will have a cigarette because they said the cravings were too strong and they gave in. Interestingly, some of these people last more than 3 days, by which point all of the nicotine has left their body. So, the apparent craving they felt was purely psychological, not physical. Nevertheless, you may want to repeat the Stop Smoking Strategy with them and then take them through the Craving Busters.

Finally, some people will continue to smoke "just because." They may not be able to put their finger on it, but the part of them that wanted to keep smoking did battle with the part that wanted to quit and the smoking part won. For such people, we recommend using the NLP technique known as *the Visual Squash*.

The following description of the technique should be enough to demonstrate its use, or provide material for a self-hypnosis recording.

The Visual Squash

Acknowledge that a part of you wants to quit smoking, but a part of you clearly wants to keep smoking.

State the negatives that you experience from smoking.

State the benefits, as there must be some or you would not have any desire to smoke.

Choose a hand to represent that desire to smoke. Place that hand out and focus on it, thinking of all the benefits you had been getting from smoking. Acknowledge that there are positive desires behind your desire to smoke and that you just need to find a better way to meet them.

Now look at your other hand and focus on it. And think of all the benefits you are going to get after you completely quit smoking. As you focus on that *really feel* all of the benefits.

Place both hands out in front of you, palms facing each other, focusing forward. As you do so, imagine that both hands in the debate can accept each other.

The part of you that wanted you to smoke, may be able to acknowledge the benefits behind why you wanted to stop. And the part of you that wants to stop may understand the desire behind the benefits from the old smoking habit.

Now imagine if the two hands could become friends, so that you could get the benefits behind your old desire to smoke, whilst also living the lifestyle and enjoying the benefits of being a non-smoker.

Imagine those hands coming together to form a new part of you.

Allow your hands to come together, of their own accord, only as quickly as you can make a single-minded decision to *quit smoking completely*.

And as those hands start to move together, you can realise that the old part that wanted you to smoke was doing so from positive, but misguided motivations.

Imagine what it would be like for both parts to work together, to allow you to enjoy all of those benefits that you were subconsciously seeking.

As those hands touch, realise that you are in a total state of congruence, a total single-mindedness to *quit smoking completely*. And as those hands touch, creating a new unified part for you, you can place your hands over your heart, as you imagine that part sinking deeper inside you, reaching into the very core of your being.

Appendix E – Help for Non-Smokers

As well as the hypnotherapy you have received, please run through these tips and hints to aid you in your new life as a non-smoker. Think of these as stabilisers, whilst you get used to the new you!

Breathe

When someone smokes, at least half of what they breathe is simply air pulled-in through the cigarette. So if you feel any cravings in the early days, you can instantly overcome them by taking three deep breaths.

Rubber Band

Talking of cravings, they are usually rare following hypnotherapy. However, some people experience them during those first 3 days when nicotine is leaving their body. So, some therapists advise wearing a rubber band on their wrist and snapping it whenever they even think about smoking. It is effective!

Why not have a Spring clean?

It is important to remove all tobacco products from your environment. Throw away ashtrays, old lighters and anything that you used to associate with smoking. The mind works by association, so it is good to remove or adjust anything that you associated with smoking.

For example, you might be accustomed to smoking in certain situations. So, if you used to smoke in the car, on the way to work, drive a different way and take some mints with you. If you used to smoke in a certain seat at home, swap chairs, or at least move them round a bit. Why not use it as an excuse to have a good old spring clean?

Take a Break – and a drink of water!

Some smokers use smoking to give themselves breaks during the day. Taking a break is good for you and it is a good idea to carry on doing so. However, find a new reason for taking time off. Have a walk around the block, have a cup of tea or drink of water. In fact, carrying a bottle of water with you will be a good habit to get in to. You may want to drink 8-10 glasses of water a day to help wash out your system.

Drink Fruit Juice

When you stop smoking, blood sugar levels in your body tend to fall. Fresh fruit juice contains fructose which restores your blood sugar levels, as well as vitamin C and high levels of water and fibre.

Reward yourself

It is a good idea to reward yourself every time that you reach a milestone. This could be the first week or first month, the six month target, or a certain level of money that has been saved.

Bibliography

Allen, R. (2000). *Scripts & strategies in Hypnotherapy*. Bancyfelin: Crown House Pub.

Battino, R & South, T. (2005). *Ericksonian Approaches.* Carmarthen: Crown House.

Carson, S., Marion, J. and Carson, S. (2014). *Quit: the Hypnotists Handbook to Running Effective Stop-Smoking Sessions*. Changing Mind Publishing.

Havens, R. and Walter, C. (2015). *Hypnotherapy Scripts: A Neo-Ericksonian Approach to Persuasive Healing*. London: Routledge.

Jensen, Mark P. (Ed.), (2017). *The Art and Practice of Hypnotic Induction*. Kirkland, WA: Denny Creek Press.

Miller, S. and Berg, I. (1995). *The Miracle Method*. New York: W.W. Norton.

Peele, S. (2006). *7 Tools to Beat Addiction*. New York: Crown.

Tiers, M. (2010). *Integrative Hypnosis*. USA: Melissa Tiers.

About the Author

Graham Old is a Solution-focused Hypnotist from the United Kingdom.

A Graduate of Spurgeon's College, London and the University of Wales, Graham is a former University Chaplain and remains an active participant of local peace and justice campaigns. He also has experience as a Father's Worker and Assistant Social Worker, as well as working in private practice.

Graham is a popular conference speaker, writer and trainer, with two decades experience teaching meditation and self-hypnosis. He is the author of the popular *Inductions Masterclass* series of books, the developer of the Therapeutic Inductions approach and co-developer of Brief Hypnosis.

Graham is the author of the fictional memoir, *Of Madness and Folly* and the developer of Plastic Spoon.

GRAHAM OLD

About the Publisher

"These novels will give way, by and by, to diaries or autobiographies—captivating books, if only a man knew how to choose among what he calls his experiences that which is really his experience, and how to record truth truly."

(Ralph Waldo Emerson)

Put like that, we at Plastic Spoon have one aim and one aim only: to record truth truly. We write fiction that offends and Self-help that actually helps. And we address issues affecting the authors themselves. We are proud to be just a little bit different.

Imagine Charles Bukowski, with an English accent, as your therapist!

So, if you are interested in books that describe, discuss or assist the struggles of ordinary people leading ordinary lives, get in touch.